Dark

Migrations

by
Richard delos Mar

9/12/93

For Connie & Dwight
A beautiful couple,
The Best always

Ranger Rick

Richard delos Blackmore

ACKNOWLEDGMENTS

These poems first appeared , sometimes in different versions, in the following publications:

Mid-American Review: "Wind Rattles"
Pembroke Magazine: "Crossties"
St. Andrews Review: "Eel Hunters"
The Glen Falls Review: "Harbor"
Mt. Olive Review: "Red Bicycle From Mother", "Whirl Again",
          "White Sleep"
The Crucible: "Snowfield"
International Poetry Review: "His Photograph"
The Greensboro Review: "Jekyll Island, 1942", "Trinity, 1945"
Expressions: "Still Life", "Assault On Breadbox Mountain"
Award Winning Poems - North Carolina Poetry Society:
        "Migrations" - Poet Laureate Award
        "Fridays" - Thomas H. McDill Award
New Horizons: "Crossties" reprinted
Manna: "Sir Dalzac of Weimar"
Anthologies - *North Carolina's 400 Years: Signs Along The Way*:
        "Duke Campus", *Weymouth*: "Harbor" reprinted, *Here's*
        To The Land: "Harbor" reprinted, *Coastal Plains Poetry*:
        "Snowfield" reprinted, "Trinity, 1945" reprinted

I S B N : 1-879934-00-0
Congress Card Catalogue No.:   TXU 472-886

Printed by: PBM Graphics
             Research Triangle Park, North Carolina

For: St. Andrews Press
             Laurinburg, North Carolina

for my wife, Bernadine

and to my three great teachers:

Lee Strasberg, *actor*
Jean Rikhoff, *novelist*
Robert Hedin, *poet*

CONTENTS

SNOW AND SMOKE

FORWARD

How about "Terrific!" Or "Splendid!" Seriously, I had encountered some of these poems singly in various outlets and had certainly appreciated both the vision and the voice, but reading the collection was another experience entirely; the poems have a cumulative effect so that the whole is indeed greater than the sum of its parts. And the parts are very good indeed. I started making notes at phrases or images or ideas that I especially liked, then, seeing that such excellence was the rule, not the exception, and not wanting to merely gush, I stopped. But thank you for giving me this opportunity.

Peter Farb has stated that in a world where human beings are constantly flooded with words, "One function of poetry is to depict the world with a fresh perception —to make it strange — so that we will listen to language once again." Richard delos Mar's poetry certainly fulfills that function: not one of these poems fails to surprise, to provide "a fresh perception" that jars us from somnolence or apathy. Reading them, we do indeed "listen to language once again" — and we will also view experience with clearer, sharper eyes. ...I look forward to seeing DARK MIGRATIONS (I like the title) done up proud, the way St. Andrews does poetry!

Sally Buckner

EARTH AND FIRE

*"...earth and sky, like two hands
cupped on a secret."*
Steven Ratiner

The Night I Was Conceived

All over Long Island,backyards
darkened; wash flapped
on the lines. Porch lights
flickered, and Philcos scratched out
"Blue Moon".

In Washington, Hoover fidgeted
with his tie, forcing the knot
tighter. Rain fell, melting
the last snow, and people
stood in bread lines,
blowing on their hands.

My father came down
from his canvases, splattered
with paint. Mother, handing him
the soap, watched as he lathered
over and over. She turned,
flicking the radio off,
the light slowly dying.

Sleeping Late

Shapes once familiar beat
Their wings, shadows
On the cave wall.

Darkness of the owl's
Folded wing,
Darkness of the forest...

Beneath the footfall
of my shoes,
Above my father's shadow
Lightning splits the cold air.

FRIDAYS

The stove simmers; clouds
boil up thunderheads, a blackness
rocks every corner of the house.

I search for a place to hide;
the lamps sway in the dark.

Outside a light breeze lifts
the wash on the lines.
The dog barks.

Room to room the winds roll
back and forth; lightning
crashes on the stairwell,
fists bang the walls.

Always the scuffing of large feet,
wreckage kicked aside.

Under the scarred dining room table,
I hear the rain splashing
over the sides. Torrents
slide down the cellar steps.

On Fridays the house lists
like a drunken ship.

Skylight

Every morning I watch his spidery hand
arc above the canvas, light
flaring off his wedding ring.
Oil paint, turpentine, Mason jars
murky with my father's brushes.

Outside, it is 1934.
They are boarding up the First
National Bank. A small boy squats
at the curb. Newspapers tangle
his legs, then blow over and over
like tumbleweed down the street.

Below, I shuffle toward the dark.
For the first time this summer
I reel in a black and glistening eel,
dust settling on the Hudson.

Snow Field

for Robert Hedin

In March they came: one hundred thousand deer
searched valleys, streets, and backyards.
Planes dropped hay. Belly deep
in snow, three gnawed our cherry bark,
mouths cut raw.

Clouds of steam rolled
from kitchen pots mixed
with the smell of Betadine.
My twelve-year-old tonsils swabbed,
my small body draped
on the enameled table. Slowly
sinking in ether,
I recalled muffled gunshots, echoing
through the dark.

That evening across the field,
trees creaked in the wind.
I saw a doe dangle
from my neighbor's oak,
a brown smudge against the sky,
her ribs hanging out,
blood dripping from her tongue.

SEPARATION GHAZALS

The surge of bruised
    v o i ce s ,
suitcases slam shut.

Restless at the mirror.
    I stare
down the long hallway.

Moonlight looms
    off the lake,
shadows bounce on my nakedness.

I can no longer feel
    the carpet,
nor smell the staleness of
    the house.

Out there, the rower
    rocks,
algae glowing on his oars.

Midwest Funnel

At dusk I drive toward a cloud
perched on a bent ribbon
of black, past restless wheat fields,
and corn rows supporting the sky.

Gathering a string of poles, my eyes
dart with each pulse beat
while dashboard lights
become the brightest stars
on the horizon.

My fingers tighten on the wheel.
Glancing in the mirror
at a twilight ridge,
I can almost make him out
through darkness, my father
waiting there, crushing
his last cigarette, smoke
clouding his face.

Crossties

In a faded gem box

I find the band,

gold twisted on gold,

disconnected,

like railroad cars

never to couple again,

Pictures of my wife in that hazy past

flash through the night window, and

my heart spins like clacking wheels,

ticking over crossties.

Red Bicycle From Mother

1907-1968

The wheels of my mind turn;
my night-light on,
and another pencil line
on the carbon
of the darkness,
breath drifting
toward the Milky Way.

Without you, I scrub floors,
seep through the cracks,
or I am dice rolling
across a table,
turning up any number.

For certain, I am color-
less without the ash
of your curls,
the blue of your dress
drawing me everywhere.

Carolyn's Trip

For my aunt

She drifted back to a Moroccan night;
a street urchin selling rugs,
chanting words like a prayer.

Her shopping trip in Hong Kong
where the swaying rick-shaws
mingle with shouts and car horns.

A Parisian restaurant with the aroma
of Chateau-Briand, chicory salad,
cafe-au-lait, and chocolate eclairs.

An evening at the black rock
of Gibraltar, warm with the Malagan
Christmas carolers singing
away the dusk.

Wavy lines on the miniature ships
mark cancelled postal stamps
from everywhere, people visited
for seventy-nine years.

She never learned to drive a car
or run a washing machine.
In December, afloat on a white sheet
her gritty words "NO intravenous!"
Carolyn pulled the connection
from her long voyage.

Whirl Again

Spinning pottery, and I,

with clay hands and kiln colors

blur deeply the baked cracks.

The wheel pushed beyond

artistic dust.

On the shelf lumps of clay

and words, spherical and flat,

drop like wind music

with rainbow colors.

Finish, study, redo: mold

the form, and whirl again,

fingers of my mind.

White Sleep

For Ron Bayes

Upright on the platen
the paper either curls
cracking like a shell
or   by placing words
becomes bound in restrictions
later found on dusty shelves

The choice is thin
like grains of fiber
rubbing themselves fragile
in parched acidity
pulped, pressed to this shape
flat as the Atlantic
the paper entices me to change
 the whiteness of myself

Geese

From Long Island, Washington,
and Michigan they gather, bobbing
on high winds, scattered
spots against the sky.

And in the dark, high over
the flickering lights of the Hudson,
they storm down
from their canvas.

When the moonlight glows
on the rower's oars, when the cold
touches summer feathers, they hurry
toward the brightest star.

Out in the darkened yard
I stand, head tilted back,
recalling her refusal to have
a son, watching my breath drift
toward the marbled clouds.

Wheels

With CLOSED signs
in my truck, I watch
the family in denim,
shoes swallowed in debris.
Overhead gulls circle
for their turn, like white
bowknots in the sky.
                    Searching
the steel bins, the boy,
with uncut blond hair, stumbles
on a wheeless bicycle. He holds it
high for his father to see.
                              Loping
with his club foot, he takes it
to an old truck where he rubs
it with a dirty rag, back
and forth, up and down, spits
on it and polishes until
the scarred red paint shines.

            When it's time
to leave, the boy carefully
lifts the bike into the back,
climbs on, pulling his leg
after him. The scarred shoe dangles.

            I hammer in
the signs, THIS LANDFILL IS
CLOSED UNTIL FURTHER NOTICE.
Sitting in the truck a while.
I imagine him with a haircut,
face scrubbed clean, leg perfect.
I hope his father finds wheels
for that bicycle.

Wind Rattles

The night I died, wind rattled

in the roof gutters.

The clouds all changed course,

and children looked up

 from their open windows.

The rains came, and lake fish

circled to the top.

Leaves flew,

and the long Kudzu bowed

toward the east.

And I lay down, sheets

rising like wings

from their lines,

lifting over the rooftops.

Richard delos Mar

WI ND AND WATER

Richard delos Mar

A Room Like A German Prison

My grandfather stooped
to tighten straps; old leather,
his olive hands white
from the weight, backpacking
supplies through Idaho in 1891.

Pushed by a biting sandstorm,
he turned back to his wayside
 room. At the window, the oak
left no space for the sky.
Shadows of limbs crept
along adobe walls.

He breathed in places
like this, unpainted and dank.
 Places where echoes of <u>achtung</u>
 tilted the walls
to a coffin of cinder blocks.

In Pocatello, this home
where he tried to mend
the cracks, his drying hands
spread like spider webs,
choking at those echoes.

The Paperweight

On winter days my grandfather
rolled it over and over,
the snow turning the ball milky.
I'd stand there, nine years old, and watch
his large hands finger it,
searching for its seams.

On such days he'd lob the glass,
and from underneath that opaque dark
the white would burst, heaven
gone mad. Slowly the flakes
drifted down, would settle on a field
so white, so still, I wanted
to walk into it, my breath
steaming in the cold.

Swimming

For Jean Rikhoff & Judy Madison

"A brebis tondue Dieu mesure le vent"

In Moline that summer I waited,
white robed, in line.
Up to his chest in the baptistry,
 grandfather crossed my arms:
shivering, water rose over my head,
bubbles rubbed my nose.
"In the name of.. "   Words,
lost in the water.

Eyes shut, I recall those small
busy globes,
each in its rubbery space,
a shaft of white foam
spent seeking its own world.
Pushed by his hand,
I dropped toward blue tile,
the sun breaking
across the pool walls.

That moonless night
on my knees in prayer,
I took the O from God,
gripped it so tight,
it broke
into the sign of the fish.

Eel Hunters

At dusk, they slithered up
the Hudson, those sweet lampreys
from their Bermuda spawn.

Boat lamps swayed
in the mist, rods flashed
high over the pilings.

Later, the long dock shone
with blood and fog, and grandfather's
breath rose cold into the dark.

On such nights I wanted to run.
He'd rock that butcher knife
back and forth, like the boats
in the Hudson's dim light.

Harbor

The day my grandfather died,
I smoked my first cigarette
squatting on hay
musty as a root cellar.
Outside, hogs
 panted in their pens,
 and far off the moonlight
glistened on miles of old fence.

At the hospital that night,
his oxygen tent
billowed like a sail, hoses
like ropes moored him to his bed.
I waited, listening
to the plastic bellows
and counted, remembering
his breath like smoke,
cold over the corn stalks.

His Photograph

For Adrienne Rich

At the bottom, he swims by the wreck.
He dreams of salvage, gold
rings flaring in the sun.
Again and again, I dive for him
my body twisting; red gilled,
fins catching bright streamers
of seaweed.

In the dark, a wall
of barnacles: I slither
in moonlight to the masthead
looking for his silhouette.
Deep down, he floats,
arms out, face gleaming
with algae.

Still Life

Next to the rife needled

Carolina pine

his unglazed vase, pock marked

in potters' gray.

Its sheared off

neck designed

to hold one rose

one rose

Leather

In my grandfather's barn, I kneel
before his steamer trunk,
its weathered tan straps, chalky
from layer on layer of harvest dust.
Inside, on the tray,
his horsehide baseball,
darkened by spit and skin oil
like the bridles overhead,
its large seams a red scar
tracking the cover, holding
back the wounds.

Now, winding up as he did
tall on the mound, I pump
and hurl it, striking
the saddle's horn above the bales.
As shafts of light mirror dust
motes in that darkness, I turn
toward the open field,
and see him there,
sitting straight on a palomino,
galloping high
over the right field fence,
fading into the frosted night.

Migrations

Pebbles in hand, I lean over the edge
dropping one at a time.
I see a reflection-
grandfather's Germanic face
staring up from the well.
                              The hidden gift
in the closet's darkest corner;
the bright canary in a darker corner.
I killed it.
I only meant to scare it, to see it fly, **a blur**
of white and yellow sailing.

                              Ceremoniously buried,
it flies from oak root to oak root,
through the veins in my head. Goldfish
swim there too, whole schools
gliding like lamplight.
                              Another stone
and grandfather's face
is a flock of geese,
and then another,
migrating home.

Richard delos Mar

SNOW AND SMOKE

"...man passes through these forests
of symbols which watch
him...

...which can sing the transfer of
spirit and senses."

Beaudelaire

Richard delos Mar

Assault On Breadbox Mountain

Along the formica abyss

      an olympian hand

sweeps him into flight

      melon morsel in tow.

Air bending

      his already bent antennae

somersaulting again and again

      in a spiral gainer;

cracking his middle body

      on the forest below.

Stunned between nylon bristled trees

      the three bodied ant shudders

six legs

      clawing at the sky.

Sir Dalzac of Weimar

The big rock place

where sometimes the orange moon

sits on the pine ridge

I stare at my dirt boots

as evergreen shadows sway

by the sandy lake edge

He freely roamed this spot

velvet ears flapping

nose sniffing

Never a day like this before

shoveling dirt on his shallow grave

Duke Campus

Page Auditorium groundswells

with Brahms, cacophony of Ives,

dissonance of Prokofiev. The North

Carolina Symphony, an immense short lived

battle. Students, with clattering steps,

attack cancer at the Medical Center,

prejudice in Divinity School

A fugue of buildings rise

high like the Chapel Tower,

low as a battle scarred classroom.

Copper kettle drums echo down

Duke's fairways. Before this stone

bulwark appeared, sweating in tobacco

fields, blacks sang gospel here,

"Rock of ages, cleft for me,

Let me hide myself..."

JEKYLL ISLAND, 1942

Three blocks from the Huddle House,
behind blackout drapes,
Misters Goodyear, Macy, and Gould
cluster, confused by what
they don't understand.
Complacency hangs like Spanish moss
from the yardarms of their yachts.
U-boats tread water,
rocking under the waves.

With their houses on leased land,
the government advises,
then raises the drawbridge,
steel mottled the color of seaweed.
First their souls flew
from the island, like gulls in a storm;
then their yachts,
yardarms piercing the sky,
crosses on a cloud.

Trinity, 1945

The Main Street marquee glows,
neon flashing over and over.
Inside, in the darkness
I wait for the white wall
of light, and from the rear
a shaft filled with specks
pierces gray smoke.
The screen explodes.

A-Bomb

July in Alamogordo: they test the ~~A-bomb~~
All day
hedgerows of clouds ripple away.
The blast reflects off goggles,
colors of crushed rainbows.
Smoke rises from the earth,
and the searing turns the sand
into lakes of shimmering glass.

Near Chosin Reservoir, Korea

The Patrol, with blood red
on their backs, uncover the cannon.
In this untouched world,
they are the only color.
Flakes of every fin shape
fell for days, as if a great
moon shed its outer layer.

Forty feet of snow created
cornices on the peaks. Echoes
of the big gun bellow down the valley.
A spray of snow at the top blows away,
showing a crater under the main
overhang. Another blast, again
a pockmark on the peak.

Vibrated loose it slides,
then rolls, gathering itself
like a wave, rips everything
in its path, and dies
at the bottom. Thirty feet
of debris, evergreens uprooted,
stick out of this gigantic
pincushion, covering
the one road out.

At The Spa

"The aim of life is to die young,
as late   as   possible." Anonymous

The oriental woman's leathery
creases of skin fall down
her face. She scrunches
that marbled look into checkered
patterns, yellow teeth glowing.
I return her smile

At the pool of hot foam,
as globules charge up my back,
I remember another face —
Lt. Lucky Collins. We left Utah,
exchanged cap and gown for U.S.
Marine starch. At paymaster
school, the dampness of night
settles on a cavernous Quonset
Hut. He'd be rolling dice, windmill
arms pumping thru cigarette haze.
Craving fortune, he picks Korea's
front lines, where money
stands for nothing. Men gamble
paychecks, hoping to forget.

Later at Treasure Island,
Lucky leans against my cash table.
A corporal guides him, takes
his back pay, carefully putting it
in his pocket. Lucky's face,
marble lined, eyes unblinking,
now a face of stone.

Richard delos Mar

Arlington

It used to be a farm.
Now no food grows,
no shade trees hold
back the grass.

Cries of bones and roots
rub together. Under
lazy clouds the white swords
stitch rows
on this green field.

In the subterranean
glow, all the boots
point to the sky.
Ribs slowly twine,
sap flowing,
to another planting.

No Word For Snow In Abu Dhabi

Feb. 28, 1987, Durham Morning Herald

The first time in recorded history
snow in Arabia, a night of twenty
inches in forty-five minutes.
Women all over town dropped
their veils. Pearl moons
crashed, their first dust
sifting like flour on the camels.
Goatherds left their stalls,
and steaming pails of milk
overflowed.

          Without stars,
those who were out covered their heads
and wandered, shuffling toward home.
Circling the miracle
a silent space
between their thoughts
spread out
among flakes,
and the unborn
shall be turned away.

About the Author

Richard delos Mar has been published in a number of magazines before this, his first full volume. Workshop leader, public reader, and award winning poet, are just a few of his many titles. Mr. Mar resides in Durham, North Carolina.